CROROCCAN HOLIDAY
Poems of a Marriage

Lauren Tivey

1st Place Winner of The Poetry Box Chapbook Prize, 2019

Editing & Book Design by Shawn Aveningo Sanders.
Cover Design by Robert R. Sanders.
Original "Moroccan Architechture" Photo by Niklas Schweinzer.

ISBN: 978-1-948461-37-5
Printed in the United States of America.
Wholesale Distribution via Ingram.

Published by The Poetry Box®, 2020
Portland, Oregon
ThePoetryBox.com

For Gerard:
Courage in the face of disease

*I lie in the middle of the road
and wait for the caravan of the mad.*

~ Abdellatif Laâbi,
"I'm a Child of This Century"

CONTENTS

Memorial

Us that day on the boat, bright-eyed and eager and gliding across the iridescent bay where the two continents arch to a kiss, rainbow spumes dashing off the prow, and the delight of leaping dolphins, and the liquescent sunlight a balm of all ills, buoyant between sanity and madness, sobriety and saturation, Spain and Morocco; on the glittering Strait of Limbo we gave ourselves—husband of the sleeping monster, wife of the many woes—to sacred waters, surrendered our troubles to the fount of all that is clean and holy, and I remember the waves murmured their response to our arrival, and the gulls cried their approval, and on the distant hill the bougainvillea drowsily nodded *yes, yes, welcome*, against the whitewashed walls of the medina, and for a moment, all was lovely, warm, and inviting in this, our crossing toward catastrophe.

Arriving Tangier

The one-legged man is begging in the road.
Nearby, a boy is punching his horse in the snout,
dutifully, with neither wrath nor glee. And
the insane woman, with her feet wrapped

in bandages, skin lesions oozing, is swathed
in a blood-red Moroccan flag which barely
covers her behind, is muttering, is following us
down a dark street, is a nightmare, a Burroughsian

terror, and we almost run. Turning the corner,
a street thief—chased, caught, beaten with a shovel.
We are far from home, and we watch, silent and grim:
it is Ramadan, and everyone is angry. For comfort

or for sport, we argue, that age-old quarrel, as the night
winds roll in, courtesy of the Strait, scattering rats, lifting
a sinister shroud off the city. In the garbage, gaunt strays
whine, as scraps of newspaper surf over broken pavement,

with some sort of grace. But there is no grace anymore;
not here, not anywhere. He begins the drinking again,
to smooth rough edges, he says, while my anxiety flares.
This is not our first time abroad—we have seen things before.

Tomorrow we will head inland, up to the Rif. We stand here
at the tip of the continent, all of Africa stretching in front of us,
sensing the rumblings of resentment shifting our marriage; that
we may not make it, that the times will try us, and break us.

He Would Have Cared

Quiet dawn, milky sunlight
casting its spears into the sleeping
medina: Chefchaouen revealed
inch by blue inch. It is azure

to indigo, and back again,
sapphire, periwinkle, and cyan—
liquid sky creeping over walls,
bathing the village and its dreamers.

My husband's eyes, cornflower blue,
rheumy in the hungover morning,
distant while I talk of Michelangelo,
the craze, the all-consuming desire

for ultramarine. In the Tiffany blue
street, his retching echoes. I want him
to know he was here. He should have
cared about this, he would have cared

before liquor colored existence—
his mind, now hidden away in a lapis
lazuli tomb, frozen in time, like
some Egyptian king, while I drag

his ghost up and down cerulean streets
of futility. I do not know what else to do;
I keep talking to fill the silence, the absence
of his presence, in a blue city beyond the sea.

Call to Prayer

There are times I imagine him dead, or
inexplicably vanished, a life my own—
I wander the souks, pretending, as he
sleeps off another bender back at the riad.

I am modest, but not too; it is the oven
of summer. Dark-eyed men selling daggers
watch me, but I am not afraid. I am free,
unfettered. All the guidebooks say

one should buy slippers in Morocco;
haggling, I pick the sparkled pair,
then sip mint tea amid the palms
of a cafe. Beggars approach, and I

share coins—something he forbids—
as a light breeze ushers in evening.
The *muezzin* begins the summoning,
minarets buzzing from all quarters,

and I am smiling in the setting sun,
tea refreshed, not thinking of his death
anymore, not even thinking of him at all,
but something like my own happiness.

Circus

He loses his mind in Jemaa el-Fna, amid
snake charmers, jugglers, fortunetellers,
jangling carts and crackling bonfires;

an inferno of over-stimulation, belligerence
boiling in his crazed eyes. Alarmed, I walk on,
knowing it's coming, building to an explosion.

The most beautiful African boy I've ever seen,
blue-black, innocent and dazzling, selling popcorn,
and my husband rejects him in the ugliest manner,

making a scene, leaving me to make apologies,
the boy's eyes wounded and pooling, and *oh*
the fight after, our screaming in the square,

surrounded by tourists and hustlers, him stomping
away, leaving me shaken, bewildered, my stomach
lurching. As the disorienting sky reels above, I feel

the stab of shame; a cruel finale to our scandalous act—
even the monkey grinder stopping to watch my soul crash
to the pavement, its shattering of a thousand crystal shards.

Haircut

I sleep to the pacifying swish of waves,
Essaouira's cheery harbor just a skip away,
but he is gone when I wake: sickening

fear grips at the thought of him wandering
drunk and confused, perhaps aggressive,
a loudmouthed ogre, loosed upon

the morning medina. His bag is still here,
empty bottles, butts overflowing the ashtray,
all his remnants of debauchery. I'm weary

of being his keeper, yet I throw on a caftan,
slide into sandals, wondering where to start,
as stoic and resolute as a hermit crab—

when the door crashes open, his triumphant
form edged in sunlight. I don't recognize him,
his proud grin, close-shaven head. A brute,

swimmingly sloshed, he declares he's gotten
a haircut, because it's a new day, and a new him,
and things are going to be different. This, I've heard

before. I say nothing: I clean up bottles, empty
the ashtray, while he marvels at his cropped head
in the mirror, trying to bring himself back.

The Other Woman

The article title reads: *Dating an Alcoholic?*
Run! I scoff at the simplicity, the logistical
impossibility. Morocco is not the place.

Look, this isn't a trick poem—we all know
booze, its myriad talents for mayhem, destruction.
We all know this is going to eventually end

in a hospital, with a jaundiced, hallucinating man,
and a defeated woman who thinks another day
will destroy her, too. So: he loves her.

He loves her more than me. He cheats on me
every day, tries to hide evidence. A story as old
as goddamned dinosaurs. I don't want him to die,

am not going to abandon him to the erratic
forces that be, yet there's a part of me
that would easily put a rabid dog down.

No escape, no running, no help. Not here
in the alien hinterlands. He continues to find her
in foreigner holiday shops, nose to the scent,

cradling her in his arms, whispering sweet nothings
into her neck, ravishing her in dark alleys, as I
stare into the distance, seething, and complicit.

Beautiful Beasts

The velocity at which a metal chair
hurtles through a space, say,
a sunny hotel room by the sea,
is in direct correlation to the well
of fury generated by its source,

which is to say, me. There is magnificence
in its arc; a slow-motion, aeronautical rise
the second after the chair leaves my grasp,
similar to releasing a frisbee, or perhaps
a single white dove, a graceful trajectory

which strikes me as ironic, as this is a missile
on a flight of rage. It does not matter that I miss
my target; the thunderous clatter of the landing,
inches from him, the astonished ring of his mouth,
the animal fear in his eyes, is satisfying enough.

We stand there in the aftermath, panting,
holding our corners, my gaze cutting,
a dangerous curve upon my lip, with
the marbled expanse between us, waves
hissing their endless movement, back and forth.

Cerberus

The villagers think I'm a witch. Of course,
they're not wrong—I traipse the lanes
in a peasant dress, with all the strays
prancing after me, giddy from food,
attention. I don't even need a piccolo.

The large black dog, a male, is an omen
of ill luck, unclean in the eyes of the locals,
and it just so happens that he's my favorite,
a goofball mutt, gangly, grinning, wagging,
sweet eyes sparking. An adolescent, surely.

He swaggers beside me, proud as a knight,
as the townspeople stare, stern and disapproving,
their lips pursed. Whatever; a dog loves me,
and whether I've summoned him from the depths
of Hell, or charmed him with kindness, is neither here

nor there. Every morning, he greets me at the riad door,
eager for our continuing mission through the underworld.
He licks my palm, his three heads bent in docility; the love
puddle of his gaze, devotion, fidelity, all that *dogness*—
I would kill for you, he says, I would do anything for you.

Case History

Mystery of a disease that doesn't look like a disease;
an illness of predisposition, perhaps wrought of genes,
or misfiring synapses, a malady of starving cells, a body
hostage to its sickness, a galloping hunger devouring
everything in its path—family, flesh, mind—activated
by childhood memory, bad weather, a bad day. It goes

like this: medically supervised detox, rehab, 12 steps,
group therapy, the healthy, the wholesome, and then
relapse, the sequence reboot. Doctors say the liver,
that cirrhotic slab of meat, won't tolerate disulfiram,
blocker of cravings, and the heart, the old bloodbag,
and the overworked kidneys, their filters destroyed,

are set to revolt. The hollow acoustics of the bath
echo every drip, keeping time with every thought;
I am enveloped by soft, benevolent warmth of tub,
right up to the neck, lucky to have found such a rarity
in this country—a blue and white tiled *en suite*, pristine
fleecy towels—and while he sleeps in the bed, oblivious,

my emotions cascade into welcoming water; grand estuaries
meeting. Of course, I didn't know all this before, what was
in store. Even though I've always been surrounded by sots;
by the lush, the souse, the swiller, the sad case, these
dipsomaniac hooch hounds of my life—father, ex-husband—
they were troublesome but functioning. And now him,

the one I love best, severe alcoholic. A pattern repeats.
My father's apparition floats high above, in trails of steam
hovering in the faint light, but this is symbolic, as my father
is still alive, but we are estranged, as per my mandate. Mean
and spiteful, he was, doing more damage than a wrecking ball.
And then the first husband, my bearded rock n' roller, my

biggest mistake, my spineless, jobless musician with a penchant,
no, a copious diet of pot-booze-opioids-groupies-and-grandiosity,
my God, those were wasted years with a Peter Pan who didn't
give a smidgen for me; and here they hover, taunting me
in a Moroccan bath of fairytale Moorish arches years later,
the phantom bastards. What head-shaking irony! Laughable karma!

And my husband, my Gerard, who came and took me away,
handled me like the porcelain cup I am, cradled my broken bits,
and glued me together again; son of a hard-drinking Scottish
clan, former Ska punk turned accountant, who once in youth
found his beloved mother on the bathroom floor, eyes staring
into the abyss, who cleaned the death muck from her body,

who watched his family members die off from the drink
and controlled his own taste for beer with a number-crunching
precision—suddenly imprisoned by a bloodline, the insatiable
call of hard liquor. I splash away the visions, the specters,
their leering faces: it is I who must dig deep for resolve,
and find a way to deny the past its due, to save him

somehow from chasm's edge. See, this is a case history
of two different children of two different alcoholics
who came together to burn away a madness, a crusade
in which one or both may not survive. I sink my head
under, my loosed scream vibrating the water,
calling to him, trying to pierce his alcoholic wall

subliminally. Like a dementia patient, he's still
in there, trying to find his way out of a maze, or
feeling blindly through a fog, following the sound
of my voice, disoriented and petrified, and I want him
back, to snatch him from—let's say—the predator's maw,
not one second too late. Is it too late? I keen, I rave.

[. . .]

Somewhere in America, my father gets booted from a bar,
and my ex beds a beauty after last call; they are swinish
and predictable. My bathwater turns cold, slimy with soap
and memories, and I rise. In the bed, a man, the only one
I have left in this world, twists restlessly: We will go on, yes.
Dropping my towel, I climb in, cleaving nakedly to our nightmare.

The Fisherman's Cat

The quarrel of lovers is the renewal of love.
~ Moroccan Proverb

Fish guts fly from the fisherman's knife
as he slices and dices atop the seawall, boats
burbling in teal harbor waters, gulls wheeling
and squealing, and my husband, raffish

in a straw hat, bends to pet the tabby
snaking around his ankles. This: amid
the pandemonium, glimpses of his former
self. His eyes are clear in the luminosity

of negative ions—sea, sun, wind—an elemental
cleansing. And the touch of fur, the happy purr;
we do not speak of it, but sit in that momentary
peace, side by side, the cat climbing his chest,

nudging his chin, while his tears freely spill.
His hands shake over the cat's sinewy lines,
to the tip of its kinked tail; animals always
get to him. Out across the ocean, leaden clouds

gather. The fisherman is packing his gear,
and the cat springs off for his master, the promise
of fish. Silent, we rise hand in hand, as cold drops
begin to pellet our bodies: it will not be long now.

Mirage

The sand whips up near Diabat,
obscuring our view, so prickly
we cover our heads with blue cloth,
Bedouin-style. His camel disappears
before my eyes, swirled in shifting beige
clouds. Every so often, a flash of cobalt
in front of me, only to be swallowed up
again, and I think, *what a shitty metaphor:*
there she goes, chasing after him
on a camel in a sandstorm. It just happens
to be true. When Hendrix visited here
back in the 60s, the locals seized on it,
mythologized every ounce they could
squeeze out, and you can't blame them—
money is money—and now the hotel
and psychedelic cafe in his honor
emerge and evaporate in the sand,
this grit that coats my sunglasses
in a sticky dust, that covers everything
with evil persistence. I fight to see him:
he dissolves, morphing into desert,
materializing anew, only to be buried,
absorbed and restored by the barrens
relentlessly, lost and found, lost and found.

The Nomad

He reclines on his dusty packs, indigo-swathed, something wild
and ancient in his look; a hawk come down from the sky, a being
still within, self-contained, like a compass pointing due North.

His wares spread before him—Tuareg Crosses, with their silver
geometry, navigation symbols of the grand Southern constellation,
to guide those lost home. I watch him place a hefty cross upon

my husband's neck, who wavers a bit in his stance, then steadies.
A scent of cinnamon wafts from the nomad's coiled scarves
as he leans in close to adjust my cross; his eyes as brilliant

as comets streaking across space. He knows the ways of the sand,
all the routes in and out of the desert, oriented since birth to cardinal
directions, how the sun burns at any moment, moods of the moon,

trailings of stars, and how slow and precise movements can safely
deliver one to a destination. After, my husband and I clasp the crosses
against our chests for weeks, feeling our way through, hoping for home.

Night of Decree

Full moon pulsing over the spice souk's clamor,
where robed women thread in and out of stalls, amid
colorful cones, umber-hued rows, and flavorful peaks,
bartering prices for cumin, ginger root, and saffron,

enterprising, chattering, these wives gathering
ingredients to quell errant husbands—it is
Lailat Al-Qadr, the Night of Decree, when
angels descend to earth, and the gates of heaven

open, when wishes are granted in secret, perfumed
rooms of candlelight. Hoopoe nails or hyena skulls
set their requests, along with a sealant of black wax,
to thwart the appetites of beaters, cheaters, and drunks.

Witch-wives, they cast their spells, chant against misdeeds,
the weak-willed and dissolute, undaunted by the wicked
sorcery of bones, or Islamic law, or any blowback, knowing
that when one marries wrong, certain measures must be taken.

Above the market, the moon lends a menacing glow;
crafty old mother, guiding her daughters' furtive work.
Tonight, it is decreed, the men will step carefully
into their homes, penitent, and earlier than usual.

Everything You Need to Know

after *The Moroccans*, Henri Matisse

The child's building blocks of the painting: circle, square, rectangle,
its dabbling in Cubism, are what draws the eye, along with the anchor
of a black background, saturated colors of orange, green, blue, pink,
minimal interference, everything but basics stripped away. I try but fail

to fully grasp the composition—some sections ambiguous. What seem to be
prostrate worshippers in the bottom left are in fact melons and leaves, laid
on a grid, for sale in the market. And though the man on the right appears
to be raising a great lobster claw, it is instead a prone figure, gleaned

from the artist's earlier sketch. Off-kilter, confused, fragmented; my mind
whirls for stability, and what does make sense is the architecture, clean lines
of the domed marabout, the window, the arch, even the pot of blue flowers. This
is how I attach logic to the world, tethering to the concrete, although I am drawn,

still, to the abstract and metaphorical. Notice there are no women, which is no
mistake. Morocco is a man's public domain, something unspoken, understood as
one wanders the medinas, women mysterious wisps of chador floating by, silent,
ever-watchful. Matisse painted this after his visits, back in *Issy-les-Moulineaux*,

needing time for it to set in his mind, before culminating in some expression,
which I find necessary, having visited during the most baffling and disturbing
time of my life; one needs to ponder, meditate, muse over Morocco, a distillation
of the senses, for a deeper knowing, a more precise account of how it transforms,

yet, is elusive. I have seen the flowerpot upon the balcony, knelt to inspect melons
at market, crept past men at their prayer rugs, meandered down arched alleys;
this black base brings everything you need to know about the country
to the fore. My experience comes into focus: its sorrows drying in the sun.

Hunger

In the date groves of Skoura, laden sprays
of ripe fruit; pendulous, bountiful. And then,
the glazed lozenge upon the tongue, soft
and erotic spurt under the teeth, syrup
sun-warmed, heady as honey, sweet as sex.

We have gorged ourselves to nausea, both of us
greedy as lovers. And what of this ravenous desire?
Of two broken people craving delights of the orchard,
or an ardent touch, our bodies eager and feverish,
even though our lives have not been perfect? Aching

in this misery of existence, we court rapture,
succumb in a frenzy of intimacy, because
we hold hope in this human flesh of ours,
and that is sometimes enough, to know
the assorted gifts of the sensual, whether

lofty or base, tender or crude. In the palms,
amber jewels hang, mature, ready to pluck,
this timing everything, before decay sets in;
we would be wise to heed its occasion. Come,
let us taste its hot kiss upon our lips, while we may.

Aberration of Starlight

Say you're zipping down the Rif mountains
in an ancient Mercedes on a moonless night,
your driver laughing into his phone, one hand
on the wheel, as the rollercoaster road lurches
you in the back seat. Let's say you're high

on hash. Let's also note that Moroccan kif
is a known face-melter: Look, outside the stars
are jumping, and the car is maybe a spacecraft;
nothing makes sense, nothing lines up, and you
don't know where you're going—oh, wait,

Fes. A turn and a dip, the weightless hover,
the oncoming headlights, the driver's eyes
flashing in the mirror, your bodhisattva
chauffer of the effluvious djellaba, somehow
smoking-talking-driving, so perhaps he's

instead djinn, and that doesn't bode well at all.
But you're being squired through the galaxy,
the extraterrestrial fells, like Martian royalty
on holiday, and your cheekbones suddenly
feel majestic and pronounced. Coming down

into the valley, the radiant city prepares for
your landing, its antennae quivering, satellite
dishes squawking your arrival: there are glad
and welcoming cries, a silver tea service, and
everything's extraordinary, everyone's a star.

Fes

Throbbing medieval city, its jumble of rooftops, lacing cables, trumpeting minarets, its stinking leather souk, horrifying vats, warren of the medina, laden mules swaying and braying, legions of humanity, their shouting, their cacophony, the garbage piles and rotting vegetables, slime underfoot, the holy spectacle of life and the revulsion too, and that one Ramadan evening, the sunset call, everyone disappearing off the streets for *Iftar*, the meal to break the fast, and suddenly the metropolis of a million deserted, down to its bones; how comically it went down—cartoonishly, or perhaps operatically, in unspoken cooperation, a dance of doors bolted, windows shuttered, every person and every animal, down to the random chicken, vanished, leaving market stalls and goods unattended, only the yellow sodium lights glaring over the abandoned souks, and then the post-apocalyptic hush of a long-dead civilization, and we wandered, marveling at the emptiness, the loneliness, inspected buildings, archways, squares, and twisting alleyways, the entire place to ourselves—Fes, in her ugly and revealing undergarments, and it was unnerving, and felt somehow forbidden and profane, and we crept away, leaving the vacant, silent city to herself, too terrified to confront the naked actuality of ourselves, all alone in the world.

The Lost Boys

Down the ochre alleys of Marrakech,
the inconspicuous riad entrance. When
I emerge, I find six lively boys, curious,

jumping this way and that. I tell them I am
a teacher, and this elicits rounds of *oohs*
and *aahs.* Skipping and piping, they follow me

out to the main road, with question after question.
When I return from shopping, I bring them a large pizza,
causing joyful mayhem, and they tear in and eat

right in the alley, their grins smeared with tomato paste.
After, they sit and rub their bloated bellies, groaning
like fat old men. This is just what I need—the hilarity,

merriment of children; always a den mother
of misfits, outcasts, and fallen angels. It makes
no difference to the world. Before retiring,

a tug at my sleeve: a wilted flower thrust at me
from a small, dirty hand, all a boy can find to give;
and to me, and to him, it matters more than anything.

Pottery Shop

Cupboards and shelves rattle as we move
through the rows of stacked ceramic dishes,
tchotchkes of gaily-painted arabesques,

while the artist throws clay on the wheel
in another room, the air lucent and warm,
dust particles floating in a sunny window.

I overhear my husband beguiling the potter
with his accent, that brogue always a surprise
to strangers, often eliciting a *Braveheart!* Or,

a discussion of family tree, ancestral history.
I poke around the pottery, listening to them, him
seeming normal at the moment, a delightful

fucking Scot, who no one knows was
an utter fiend the day before yesterday.
I shake my head—he would've been booted

from here in a drunken state, the proverbial
bull in a china shop, yet here he is, like the
second coming of MacGregor, a tartan-smart charmer,

with a lilt to die for. Suddenly beneficent, he tells me,
get whatever you want, with a sweep of the hand,
as if I didn't know what a miser he is. I let him go on,

having his act, his spotlight of adoration—God
knows, he hasn't gotten it from me of late. I pick
the large, glazed dish with beaming sun face, all

blues and yellows, scalloped edges, easily the most
expensive thing; of course, it's not going to make it
home, and you can guess whether that's my fault, or his.

All the Soft Things

In a shadowy alcove of the casbah wall,
a slight, mud-caked cat, too lethargic
to mewl. Her dull eyes, her prominent
rib cage—she's nearing death, and no one

stops to look. We smuggle her into the riad
then wash her in the sink, loads of crud, bugs,
as she shivers in our palms, this frail being.
We cannot save everything, we know,

but we must try. We must always try.
She refuses milk, a bit of meat, even water,
but settles into the warmed towel; concerned
as new parents, we rise through the night

to check for faint signs of breath, a cloak
of doom weighing our movements. *Please,*
just this one thing, we say. In the morning,
the silent, still bundle, which destroys us.

In tidal pools below the city, we bury her
in a sandy spot protected by rocks. A stray
feather from me, a handful of pebbles from him:
Llay-haf-tik, we say, *may God bless you.*

Waves pound the rocks, and soon, the tide's
work will seal her among the shells—our waif,
our wreckage—sheltered forever. And us? We have
learned to accept these daily sorrows as they come.

A Bar in Casablanca

Always, these foreign characters
trying to seduce me with their looks
across scarred wooden tables, haze
of smoke and slanted light, whenever

my husband leaves for the john, as if
I'd any romance left to give, as if
I were that carefree. I'm not without
bad habits: I quaff beer, puff away,

Dragon Lady in scarlet silk, bangled
wrists, treacherous of eye, and mean
with experience. Appearances, of course.
I've thought of other men, it's true,

of late the one back home, his kind face,
his bookish ways, but I've enough trouble
with the husband, a raging hurricane
of problems. The bartender refills my glass,

yet I've grown tired of the stale taste
of beer, bars, men. There are better things
to do. Perhaps I've grown old, cantankerous—
wouldn't you? I've not even a half-hearted,

conspiratorial wink left for my intrepid suitor
across the bar. Aloof, I spark another cigarette,
jangling caution his way, to leave me be, while
I contemplate the swirling tempest of my life.

Soused Sestina

A blotto fantasia, on the rocks

Picture a man whose sole motivation is a bottle,
someone aimless and roaming in a dark forest of liquor,
a wolf on his track, brambles upon the path to his lover,
hunters lurking in tree stands, guns trained on this drunk
stumbling through thorny underbrush, in need of an angel
to guide him toward the shining, boozy beacon of ecstasy;

you can imagine when he lands on the spot, the ecstatic
guzzling of amber liquid—fluid of life—in the bottle
clean and glinting, its sloshing contents, his very own angel
promising relief and comfort, freedom from fear via liquor,
an escape from reality, imaginary threats. After he's drunk
and satiated, the staggering and rolling: he's never been so in love.

Nothing matters other than being smashed, his smashing beloved;
it's a match made in heaven, the one true meaning, this ecstasy
of ethanol, forest now a seaside resort, conjured from the drink,
wonderland of waves, sun, salt, and suds, ships in a bottle,
even hunters morphed into mermaids, gesturing with liquor
from boulders in the undulating ocean, like pure angels.

It's the promised land, he's made it, and from every angle
it's clear sailing with the Seven Sisters, a balmy day, so lovely,
in boats of booze, whiling away the time, answering liquor's
siren call, forgetting past, present, and future, only this ecstasy
in his companion, his soulmate, enchanting inamorata in a bottle,
fulfilling every need and desire, which is only to be drunker

than the next lamo wobbling their way down an alley, drunk
as a skunk. *Hold fast!* he shouts, *hold true! My darling angel
I'll never leave you!* He's the chosen of the genie in the bottle,
he knows, never learning she always strands her unwitting lovers
on the rocks, battering and breaking them in sadistic ecstasy,
leaving them quivering, devoid of hope, of joy, of liquor—

[. . .]

and here he lays, once again, exposed in the sun, leaking liquor
out of every pore, buzz evaporating, no longer the drunken
sailor, baking on the crag like a crab out of water, ecstasy
turned agony, and then comes the chuckling albatross, no angel
saving him, but shitting on him as he keens for his lost love,
just a wretched tosspot withering in the glare, sans bottle.

And so his tryst with liquor ends, not with a perfect angel
blissfully drunk in his arms, but a thieving, maniacal lover,
pilfering his ecstasy, unhappily-ever-after, with a bottle.

I Find Books

Librairie des Colonnes, Tangier

Wandering among the shelves, I suddenly remember
my enraged, drunken father, who'd hurled my doll carriage
filled with books, which I'd been pushing around the house,

at four years old; even then, a bibliophile—not dolls, but
books! I'd been devastated. That he'd subject *my books*
to such treatment, something I so cherished, broke my

pint-sized heart. Now a college teacher of literature, a writer
and poet, in my element, I think, *my father can go to hell*,
and maybe that's my next book title. I've made my way

here alone, to the bookstore of Bowles, expat Beats, more
at peace now than in weeks. Surrounded by books, with
no other customers, a clerk busy at the computer up front—

I can relax and browse. I run my fingers along smooth,
uncracked spines of a row, lingering over *Ulysses*,
Don Quixote, and my favorite, *Anna Karenina*. A rich

vanilla aroma permeates the shop, the lighting and air
velvet, muted. I think of my father's literary tastes, leaning
toward political thrillers, murder mysteries, nothing deeper,

nothing Classic, nothing I could ever talk to him about.
That's it, see—we'd nothing in common other than bloodline.
He never once bought me a book, took me to a library, a bookstore,

never once mentioned my remarkable love of books
and reading, this consuming passion in my life. And though
that was the least of his sins, it was the one that hurt the most.

Petit Socco

And so, time and decay does its work on us all:
the brothel across the way, its prostitutes and johns,
the merchants, with their shopfronts and carts,
pedestrians going about their business, drug dealers,
addicts, police, tourists, animals; we're a sorry lot.

If I am (as he says) *a cunt*, ruining his fun, it's because
I have to be, have to play wicked witch to his adolescent
alcoholic fantasy, his shenanigans, his chaos, to ensure
he makes it out of this alive, the constant worry a corrosion
wearing me down, aging me by the day. But something

for me: I sit here, sipping coffee in the infamous little square,
writing poems, a literary drifter, as planned in my original itinerary,
digging a Beat scene, old Cafe Tingis, crumbling *fin de siècle*
architecture, imagination run wild with espionage, double agents,
the white-suited expats and their decadence, those long gone,

their legendary bones now disintegrating under a ceiling of dirt.
There's an attentive waiter, ruffling of newspapers. The Arab world
files past, while stray dogs beg at my feet—it could've *only* been
this, you know? Instead of this senseless extravaganza he's conducted.
I've watched with horror as our lives have frayed, unraveled, but that's

nothing new in the history of the world, or in the history of couples,
and I suppose Morocco is used to ruin—*nothing to see here, move
along*. I may be a killjoy, a glorified babysitter, but at least I've got
this teeming square, this moment of my own, this bitter poem, while
I witness our slow and pathetic slide toward a conclusion of some sort.

The Math of It

But I want to know when
to give up on someone. Time,
date, and place. Tell me that—
how much pain to endure
in the name of love? Show me
an algebraic formula, calculations,
a litmus test, a pie chart, or
a spreadsheet of points logged + / -
and yes, even a Venn diagram
will do. Can it be measured
in empty bottles? A laundry list
of injuries and embarrassments?
Tell me, at what point does one
cut their losses? Surely, someone
must've figured this out by now.

Four Bare Walls

I can feel it building, this aura of tension, like
a far-off storm gathering; his darkening mood,
curt answers, shifty-eyed attention. He steals away
while I shower. I stand dripping in the tiled chamber,

sensing stillness in the suite, calling out to an echo
of my own voice. There's that moment between realization
and heartache, a second of disbelief that it's happening again.
I choke back a moan, and with slow, fastidious movements,

begin toweling off. After, in the empty room, four bare walls:
there's refuge in parameters—physical or mental—when under
duress, sometimes the only thing holding me together. Dressed,
I sit in silence upon the bed, motionless, not waiting for him,

but thinking, taking stock, counting the days until we leave,
formulating strategies to extricate myself from the heaping, stinking
mess of my marriage. Survival: emotions on hold, as I don't have
the current luxury. Cold and rational—this is how I get through.

Himself

You must suffer me to go my own dark way.
~ Robert Louis Stevenson

1. Edge

a'ways tae same shite
ev'ry day, loik tae woife's me
ma er mebbe tae fookin' boys
in blue er sumpin', cuttin' me doon
fer drinkin' loik em a wee yin,

a'ways findin' me stash an
doompin' it doon tae toilet
er tae sink—i sware tae woman's
got tae nose fer huntin' doon
tae booze, 'tis a coonstant

battle 'tween oos and tae bitch
will nae give an inch, yellin'
loik a banshee, er with her sad,
sad eyes, an i'm always tellin' her,
jes a wee bit, take off tae edge, ya?

an now she's got oos inna
dry coontry fer tae holiday.
tat's roight, tae wicked witch
brooght me tae a mooslim coontry
at ramadan, an i ask ye, wot kinna

evil shite is this? i'm jes as mooch
a bludhoond fer tae booze as she, an
can hoont it doon. marrrk me worrrds,
i've me ways, an 'twill foind wot i need,
an if'n she woont allow it, then fook her.

[. . .]

~ 37 ~

2. Ma

i ain't never seen 'em like that a'fore,
her cat's eyes marbled in death,
bright blue, loik maybe marine
er dook blue, i guess ye'd call it,

an they was lookin' at tae sky,
well, tae roof, anyways, when i
walked in, an there was odor
comin' from her, and sumpin'

nae right, an i sed ma, ma, ma
an she was silent an still, tae room
quiet as a crypt, indeed, aye,
i knew it. an i called tae medics

an i called my brothers, lookin'
at her prone on tae floor, an i
dint cry, i jes stared, an then
a'fore they arrived i had tae

do it, ye know, close 'em,
put a penny-fee fer tae ferryman,
an 'twas tae hardest thing i ever
had tae do, an her eyes was

so wide an glazed loik blue ice,
an her lids felt loik paper, but
they shoot, an i was lookin' aboot,
an i knew i had tae clean her up

a'fore tae boys came, i dint
want 'em all lookin' at her
loik that, an i dint want to
but it had tae be doon, an

i did, cus me poor ma
deserved her dignity,

an i worked quick, not
lookin' at her, jes doin'

wot had tae be doon,
me an her body, all 'lone
in tae quiet house, an still
i never cried over me ma,

i jes did wot i had tae,
an t'was tae worst day—
i was jes a boy, an i caint ever
ferget me ma's dead eyes.

3. Detox

tae giant bat wings of flappin' fear,
tae filthy rats in tae snickerin' shadows;
so it begins—tae shakes, sweats, cramps,
retchin', roons—an ye hate it fer wot
it's doon to ye, is doin' to ye, an ye
swear ye'll never tooch it agin, an ye
lay there terrified, unmovin', cravin' it,
but tae cramps are kickin' ye in tae gut,
those agonizin' cramps, loik hellfire an
damnation, an ye cramp and ye cramp
in places yer body should nae cramp,
an when ye shite ye cain't even reach
yer shaky hand 'round to fully clean yerself
because of tae cramps, an after ye lay quiverin'
on yer side so tae soil does nae soak through yer shorts
an stain tae bedsheets, but ye can nae sleep anyhow,
an ye can nae sit, so ye smoke, but the coughin'
sets off more cramps, so maybe ye take a wee shower,
but ye panic steppin' in tae tub, because yer balance
is shot, and ye hafta grab tae wall loik some
batter'd ole man, an when ye put tae shampoo
in an close yer eyes, tae room spins an ye almost fall—
a wee child could push ye over, yer so weak—and ye exist

[. . .]

in this agonizin' time bobble with each moment an hoor,
an even tae clockhands tickin' an tockin' tis excruciatin',
an ye cain't get out o'yer head an tae sickness will nae end,
an worst t'all is tae hurt look on tae wife's face, an ye'd
rather be homeless than see that disappointed look agin
in her eyes. fookin' christ, fookin' god, jes make it stop.

4. Mr. Whatsit

tae guilt, tae searin' guilt, fer fooksake wot
'ave i doon now, an she tells me, an her voice
is so quiet an level, loik it li'trally hurts her
tae be speakin' it, and i'm ashamed, feelin'
a good bit loik a murder'r er some sick paedo,

but also me mind's clearin' an tae shakin's over,
an tae sun's shinin' an maybe, i think, i can
stay sober fer a wee bit, jes til we get oot
o'this god-fersaken coontry, wit it's random
scooters an chickens an endless hollerin', loik

why all tae hollerin' in this coontry? Noise
coonstantly. anyway, i dint mean tae do this
agin tae her, aye, tae me. i'm loik fookin'
dr. jekyll an mr. whatsit? tae beast in me
an tae hoonger too strong, an i caint keep

woondin' her, jes loik her da an her ex,
nae better'n em a'tall. i used tae be good,
a tight scot, ya, but a good man wit decent
morals, but tae war in me's changin' me—an
tae woife, she will nae go, an i luv her fer't

an i'll rehab agin an agin if'n she wonts.
but *tae blooud in me*...aye, it's taken my
sister, my brother, my da, these genetics
nae friend tae anyone. i tell her—*roon, lass,*
save yerself, a'fore i'm tae death of ye.

In Other Words

I remember, before all this began, that starswept
midnight in another land, coming over the mountain,
stopping at the sight of the high lake glistening, Orion
reflecting his diamond-studded belt on its surface, snow
gleaming, crunching underfoot, and how we clenched
gloved hands, watched clouds float from our elated
conversation; he knelt and asked to marry me. Life

did that—offered up the enchanted moment, fired up
the smoke screen, did its dance of a thousand veils,
whispered words like *cherish, adore, protect*, charmed
the senses into submission, and since I was a romantic,
(which is another word for goner), I said yes on that
mountain, chose him, chose us, chose the future, its
many hat tricks. And so, here we are. Listen, I'm done

apologizing for my anger and exasperation, or
justifying my grief. How were we to know
that within a decade, vows we swore, the home
we'd built of each other, would collapse? I try
to hold the therapist's words close: *Disease.
Illness. Sickness. Affliction.* I catalog clear truths:
no physical abuse, no infidelity, no vicious intent...

I've not given up on the mountaintop, not yet,
and who's to say we won't make it back there,
across desert and sea, past cities and towns, up
long, winding roads through towering firs, to icy
elevations where the core of us remains, frozen
and solid and pure, preserving the words *support,
patience, recovery,* and remarkably, *hope.*

A Traveler's Lament

We are allowed to be dark after all we have seen:
we carry our bundles of suffering wrapped carefully,
say, twined in brown wax paper, perhaps in a worn
knapsack, or a locked box. Sometimes it is the weight

of a fetus, sometimes an entire planet. We move
from destination to destination, one safe harbor
to the next, cradling our cargo, its ugly contents,
shattered worlds, and burning memories, until the time

is right for release. We know exactly what it holds,
and we know it must be opened; its shrieks and wraiths
freed, its pain exposed to the light. It is a heavy load
to lay down, these tribulations of the spirit, but we know

we cannot keep packing it from place to place, for the rest
of our lives. It is acceptable to set it down all at once, or
little by little, as long as we learn to open it, and let it go.
Purified, unburdened: it is the only way to continue on.

The Journey Back

Out of the Gare du Nord, the morning express,
première classe: I am tan, fit, Bohemian,
a hardboiled survivor, prepared for any number
of troubles to unfold. *C'est la vie.* We are all
traveling to, through, or out of something, eh?
One could even say moments of gladness exist.

The car sways along its tracks, blurred landscape
flashing by—for now, I will daydream, book at my
breast, given over to emotional fatigue. Later, at the riad,
the sun will set over the rooftop, for a gardenia-scented
evening in chaise lounges; a day's end without incident.
Steaming tajines will arrive to bolster our strength, then

we will saunter in the garish souks, just a normal couple
on holiday. He will be relaxed, complacent, even
content, somewhere before the anxiety of craving, well
before the havoc of inebriation, and the snug coils of my
worry will slacken, if for a moment or two. He will
buy me orange blossom ice cream, caramelized walnuts,

and we will stop to listen to a street musician. Our love
this night will be deliberate, luxurious, under the flutter
of white gauze drapes, our bodies recalling one another's
touch, tracing map lines back to the source of something
that once was. It will be like this, and I suspect you will
indulge me here, as you know just how much has been lost.

ACKNOWLEDGMENTS

Earlier versions of some poems in *Moroccan Holiday* were previously published as a feature in the Summer 2017 issue of *Third Wednesday*, Vol. X, No. 3:

"Memorial"

"Arriving Tangier"

"He Would Have Cared"

"Call to Prayer"

"Circus"

"The Other Woman"

"Haircut"

"Beautiful Beasts"

"The Fisherman's Cat"

"Mirage"

My thanks to Cassandra Mainiero for suggestions and valuable editing help, and to Soraya Boubia for clarifying certain Moroccan customs.

PRAISE FOR
MOROCCAN HOLIDAY

In this stunning collection of finely wrought poems, Lauren Tivey writes of a holiday with deep pain and small joys. The speaker takes us on a journey of trauma as her husband relapses into alcoholism during the vacation, and tells of her difficult responses to his behavior. His disease of unrelenting suffering transforms the couple. He is, she says, "...a brute / swimmingly sloshed..." and she wonders if she can "...save him / somehow from chasm's edge." She writes "I keep talking to fill the silence, the absence / of his presence, in a blue city beyond the sea." The poems are, in fact, brilliantly alive with shades of blue, some bright and cheery, and others darker, more sinister. As this couple journeys, she is wracked with agony, though the speaker does find momentary happiness that her husband's "...eyes are clear in the luminosity / of negative ions—sea, sun, wind—an elemental / cleansing." These poems pull the reader in with their heartbreaking urgency, history, and quests. Deeply moving, always expressing complex ideas in radiant language and astonishing details, *Moroccan Holiday* is a must-read book that sings the duality of love and estrangement.

~ Virginia Chase Sutton, author of *What Brings You to Del Amo*

These poems, gathered so astutely in *Moroccan Holiday,* have such exquisite and crisp detail that they will haunt you for a while. "Circus," "The Nomad," and "Hunger" are a few perfect examples, among the many in this book, of poems that will take you by the throat and choke you with their undeniable power and brilliance. Rich images, lyrical lines that are relentless in their beauty. These poems resonate with a lush wickedness of the tongue "of two broken people craving delights of the orchard" and the bitterness of people who've had to battle alcoholism and marriage and love for a long while. "I've grown tired of the stale taste of beer, bars, men. There are better things to do." These are magnificent poems written against the backdrop of our crumbling world, Morocco, and beyond.

~ Virgil Suarez, author of *90 Miles: Selected and New Poems*

[. . .]

Written with startling poignancy and richness, Lauren Tivey's collection of poems, *Moroccan Holiday*, narrates a couple's troubled voyage to a place "used to ruin," seesawing between the splendor of its setting and the upcoming catastrophe into the depths of alcoholism and its legacy. The book starts "on a boat...gliding across the iridescent bay" on way to holiday, and quickly thrusts us into the precipice of Tangier, with its one-legged beggar, insane woman with oozing skin lesions, and scattering rats, which parallels their descent and struggle to prevail, as individuals and as partners. The poet asks, "I want to know when / to give up on someone." The reader is left pondering this and other brutal questions, but it is clear that "moments of gladness exist." Tivey's work is a compelling case study, both fascinating and surprisingly compassionate, absolutely worth reading.

~ Carolina Hospital, author of *Key West Nights and Other Aftershocks*

Travel and travail share a common root, revealing at a deep linguistic level that to journey is to suffer. Change and transformation are by nature difficult. The travelers in *Moroccan Holiday* do indeed go far, traversing physical continents and emotional minefields. Lauren Tivey is an uncanny poet, conjuring metaphor and image to convey the tale of a husband and wife at the edge of love's limit, where they are pushed by his relapse into alcoholic toxicity. The weight of their pasts and the exhaustion of carrying it all provide a sharp contrast to the cinnamon-scented streets and lush-laden markets of Morocco that would otherwise have beguiled them. The poems deliver a mix of seduction and despair, sorrow and enchantment (so many names for blue in this heady place). Through travel and travail, the woman and man somehow endure, learning how to lay down the burdens handed to them long ago and to take delight in the pleasures of their precarious present.

~ Holly Iglesias, author of *Sleeping Things*

Lauren Tivey's *Moroccan Holiday* is a gorgeous, heartrending blue tempest that charts the roughhousing of addiction in a dry land with rich diction, depth, intelligence, and awareness. Despite tumult, the center never wavers, clear among the significant lost boys, the poems' hope and generosity rising like Morocco's pink wild roses and, yes, they do make a "difference to the world."

~ Liz Robbins, author of *Freaked*

ABOUT THE AUTHOR

Lauren Tivey is the author of four chapbooks, most recently *Moroccan Holiday*, which was the winner of The Poetry Box Chapbook Prize 2019, and *The Breakdown Atlas & Other Poems* (Big Table Publishing Company, 2011). Tivey is a Pushcart Prize nominee, and her work has appeared in *Connotation Press*, *The Coachella Review*, and *Split Lip Magazine*, among dozens of other web and print publications in the U.S. and U.K.

After much international travel, including a six year stint living in China, she now resides with her husband, and a little black cat named Poppet, in a cottage surrounded by flower gardens in St. Augustine, Florida. She teaches English and Creative Writing at Flagler College.

Tivey can be reached at her writing blog:

https://laurentivey.wordpress.com

ABOUT THE POETRY BOX
CHAPBOOK PRIZE

In 2018, The Poetry Box introduced their annual Chapbook Prize competition, awarding publication to at least one poet. The contest is open to both established poets and emerging talent alike, and the editors reserve the right to select more than one poet's manuscript for publication. Currently, the contest is open to poets residing in the United States and is open for submissions each year during the month of February.

2019 Winners

First Prize:
Moroccan Holiday by Lauren Tivey (FL)

Second Prize:
Hello, Darling by Christine Higgins (MD)

Third Prize:
Falling into the River by Debbie Hall (CA)

2018 Winners

First Prize:
Shrinking Bones by Judy K. Mosher (NM)

Second Prize:
November Quilt by Penelope Scambly Schott (OR)

Third Prize (tie):
14: Antología del Sonoran by Christopher Bogart (NJ)
Fireweed by Gudrun Bortman (CA)

CPSIA information can be obtained
at www.ICGtesting.com
Printed in the USA
BVHW030427231219
567543BV00001B/19/P

9 781948 461375